The AI

How to Live and Succeed in a World Driven by AI

Koso Brown

Copyright 2024© Koso Brown

All rights reserved. This book is copyrighted and no part of it may be reproduced, distributed, or transmitted in any form or by any means, including photocopying, recording, or other electronic or mechanical methods, without the prior written permission of the publisher, except in the case of brief quotations embodied in critical reviews and certain other non-commercial uses permitted by copyright law.

Printed in the United States of America

Copyright 2024© Koso Brown

Contents

Introduction 1

Chapter 1 3

AI's Transformative Potential..................................... 3

Chapter 2 7

Important steps you should take to get ready for a world driven by AI. 7

Chapter 3 14

The danger we encounter while thriving in an AI-driven world 14

Chapter 4 30

Techniques for Reducing Artificial Intelligence-Related Risks 30

Final Thought 40

Introduction

The rapid development of AI has raised both enthusiasm and fear. The advancements in AI excite some people while alarming others. Many people these days are asking themselves questions like "Will robots take our jobs?" and "How should we prepare for the future?" It makes perfect sense given that, in terms of AI, we're all in a new situation.

AI is unquestionably influencing the nature of work in the future, altering a wide range of professions and even those that we once considered to be unassailable. Due to AI technologies' superiority in repetitive, tedious work, jobs involving them are most likely to be automated. However, it goes beyond these monotonous roles. Not all occupations are safe, even those involving human interaction or specialized training.

AI is being used by physicians to diagnose illnesses more precisely and by attorneys to review court materials more quickly.

Although this change may seem frightening, it's

important to realize that AI's development does not portend the end of human work.

Rather than serving as a substitute, AI can be a useful tool. Additionally, as AI advances, new professions like AI Ethicists and Prompt Engineers are being created that we never would have imagined. Therefore, although AI will surely have an impact on our careers, it is not only a threat. Humans have the chance to take advantage of this technology, increase our productivity, and produce amazing things.

Chapter 1

AI's Transformative Potential

Before the social viral effect of ChatGPT hits our feeds at the beginning of 2023, let's first realize that the power of AI to learn and make decisions has already had a profound impact across numerous sectors and industries. For example:

- ❖ AI algorithms are used in the entertainment industry to assist consumers receive personalized content. These are truly remarkable inventions with great potential for the advancement of humanity. However, issues will always arise with any change.
- ❖ AI algorithms are already able to diagnose illnesses more accurately than human physicians in certain cases.
- ❖ Robots powered by AI are optimizing assembly lines in manufacturing and increasing output.

The Changing Workplace Environment

The possible influence of AI on sizable segments of the labor force is one of the major worries regarding the widespread use of AI, which we have also observed in some of our patient presentations in our psychological practice. In terms of automation, for instance, AI systems are increasingly handling jobs that were previously the responsibility of humans. For instance, in the industrial sector, an AI-powered assembly line may eventually eliminate the need for manual labor.

While this may be the case, it's important to remember that artificial intelligence (AI) also can open up a wide range of new job and career prospects. Robotic engineers, data scientists, and AI experts are in more demand. Furthermore, as we become more aware of how AI is used in our daily lives, we will be able to eliminate countless hours of tedious, time-consuming work that repeats itself, freeing us up to concentrate on more significant and creative (rewarding) projects. Thus, all is not lost, but we must look for the benefits that apply to each of us personally and stay ahead of the curve

Implications for Mental Health and Ethical Issues

There are moral conundrums associated with the introduction of AI into society. The main topics of conversation include issues with data privacy, algorithmic biases, and the ethical responsibility of AI judgments. Moreover, our mental health may be impacted by the anxiety and uncertainty that come with the quick speed at which AI is developing. People who discover that their talents are becoming outdated may get anxious about their employment prospects.

The Bright Side: Embracing Human Resourcefulness

It's crucial to remember that AI cannot replace the intrinsic human abilities of empathy, creativity, and sophisticated decision-making, despite these legitimate and legitimate worries. These abilities are always in demand, which is what makes us valued members of a healthy society in addition to being human. Therefore, the true issue is how humans accept AI's power and then figure out how to live well in this new era of technological innovation.

Chapter 2

Important steps you should take to get ready for a world driven by AI.

Investing in AI Training and Education

Investing in education and training centered on AI technologies is essential for both professional and personal development in the ever-changing field of artificial intelligence.

You ought to learn how to make use of AI prompts. Everyone will start using AI to simplify daily life, so you should get on board. You'll undoubtedly shine at work if you start learning how to take advantage of AI prompts.

This could be taking courses on artificial intelligence (AI), gaining machine learning and data science certifications, or going after graduate degrees in AI Related fields.

A solid foundation in artificial intelligence and continuous learning about its developments allow people to establish themselves as authorities in the field and access a wide range of innovative and career-advancing options.

Creating a Community in the AI Field

Developing a network within the AI community can be very helpful for thriving in an AI-driven society. It implies that you need to build trustworthy relationships.

AI will never be able to replicate the human connection; therefore, you should take advantage of that. Make use of your systems administration and interpersonal skills to form connections that will further your career and open up a world of opportunities.

To offer chances for information exchange, teamwork, and mentoring, you must regularly interact with experts, scholars, and AI enthusiasts. Individuals can stay up to date on the newest advancements in AI, gain access to invaluable resources, and establish relevant contacts that can accelerate their professional growth in the field by taking part in industry events, online forums, and projects centered around AI.

Accepting Ethical Aspects in AI

It is crucial to think about the ethical ramifications of AI use as it begins to pervade many facets of our lives. Adopting a deliberate and responsible approach to the development and application of AI technologies is essential for thriving in an AI-driven world. Ethically automate your laborious tasks. Whether or not you can reduce the time you spend planning, researching, writing, or analyzing, using AI to automate repetitive and boring chores at work will free up more time for you to work on projects that interest you.

This entails guaranteeing that the advantages of AI are available to all societal sectors and advancing equity, accountability, and transparency in AI systems. People may help create a more equitable and sustainable AI-driven society by actively participating in conversations on AI ethics and supporting ethical AI practices.

Working Together with AI Systems

People should work with AI systems to improve their productivity and decision-making rather than viewing it as a danger to their job security. Artificial Intelligence is skilled at processing and interpreting large datasets, offering insights, and automating repetitive operations.

People can improve their skills, expedite processes, and concentrate on elements of their work that bring value by utilizing AI tools and platforms.

By empowering people to reach greater levels of performance and efficiency, this collaborative method can hasten their professional development.

Developing an Adaptive and Agile Mentality

People who want to prosper in an AI-driven environment where technology is advancing quickly need to have an agile and adaptable attitude. Obtain positions that satisfy your needs overall, even if your current career isn't fulfilling you.

AI can help you jointly find jobs that align with your skills, background, and interests. It can also help you prepare for interviews, automate job applications, and polish your resume and cover letter.

This entails adopting new technology, remaining adaptable, and always improving one's skill set. Individuals may position themselves at the vanguard of technological innovation and propel their personal and professional progress in tandem with AI advancements by continuing to be adaptable, proactive, and flexible in learning and adapting to evolving trends.

Promoting Critical Thinking and Creativity

Though AI is highly proficient at handling large volumes of data and accurately doing repetitive tasks, human abilities like creativity, critical thinking, and emotional intelligence continue to be extremely valuable.

Individuals should concentrate on developing these distinctively human abilities that robots cannot imitate if they are to prosper in an AI-driven world. In an AI-dominated world, people with creativity and critical thinking can approach problems in novel ways, come up with creative solutions, and adjust to changing circumstances.

Recognizing AI's Effect on Industries

To succeed in a world driven by AI, one must have a thorough awareness of how AI is affecting different industries. AI is changing conventional methods and establishing new ones in a variety of fields, including smart manufacturing, personalized marketing, and precision treatment in healthcare. People can find possibilities to employ AI in their respective fields and spur innovation by keeping up with these breakthroughs.

Furthermore, influencing AI's appropriate and sustainable integration into various industries requires an awareness of the ethical and societal ramifications of the technology.

Accepting Ongoing Education and Upskilling

Developing a mindset of ongoing learning and skill development is one of the essential strategies to prosper in an AI-driven future. As AI automates ordinary tasks, people will increasingly need to acquire complementary skills to work with AI technologies.

This could entail getting to know AI systems, comprehending what they can do, and using them to improve decision-making and productivity.

Additionally, mastering data analysis, machine learning, and programming languages can let people collaborate with AI systems, which can lead to new job prospects and improve professional development.

Chapter 3

The danger we encounter while thriving in an AI-driven world

The voices cautioning against the possible risks of artificial intelligence are becoming more and more prominent as AI becomes more advanced and pervasive.

"We need to worry now about how we prevent that from happening," stated Geoffrey Hinton, who is regarded as the "Godfather of AI" for his groundbreaking work on machine learning and neural network algorithms. "These things could get more intelligent than us and could decide to take over." Hinton said in 2023 that he was quitting his job at Google to "talk about the dangers of AI," adding that he even regrets the work he has dedicated his life to.

Unease is prevalent on several fronts, including the growing automation of some jobs, racially and gender-prejudiced algorithms, and autonomous weapons that function without human supervision.

And our understanding of AI's true potential is still quite limited.

A few of these dangers are enumerated below:

AUTONOMOUS SELF-AWARE A.I.

Concern also arises that artificial intelligence (AI) could develop so quickly that it will become sentient and operate independently of humans, potentially in a malevolent way. There have already been some reported cases of alleged sentience. One well-known example comes from a former Google developer who claimed the AI chatbot LaMDA was sentient and conversed with him in a human-like manner. Cries to halt AI development are growing louder as the field's next major milestones include creating systems with artificial general intelligence and, eventually, artificial superintelligence.

DECLINE IN HUMAN IMPACT

In certain spheres of society, an over-reliance on AI technology may lead to a decline in human influence and functionality. For example, using AI in healthcare could make people less empathetic and rational. Furthermore, using generative AI in creative projects may limit human expression of emotion and creativity. Over-interaction with AI systems may potentially lead to a decline in social and peer communication abilities. Therefore, even though AI can be very useful for automating routine jobs, others wonder if it could limit human intelligence, social skills, and sense of community.

CRISES IN FINANCE CAUSED BY AI ALGORITHMS

The banking sector is now more open to integrating AI technology into routine trading and financial procedures. Therefore, the next big financial catastrophe in the markets may be caused by algorithmic trading.

Although AI algorithms aren't influenced by human judgment or feelings, they also don't account for market interdependence, context, or human emotions like fear and trust. subsequently, at a breakneck speed, these algorithms execute thousands of trades, which they subsequently sell for meager gains a few seconds later. Market volatility and abrupt falls may result from investors being scared off by the sale of thousands of trades.

Reminders of what might happen when trade-happy algorithms go crazy include the 2010 Flash Crash and the Knight Capital Flash Crash, regardless of whether rapid and huge trading is deliberate or not. That being said, AI is not without use in the finance industry. In actuality, AI algorithms can support investors in making better, more knowledgeable choices in the marketplace. However, financial institutions must ensure that they comprehend the decision-making process of their AI systems. Before implementing AI, businesses should think about whether it gives them more or less confidence to prevent inciting investor anxiety and causing havoc in the financial system.

REMOTE WEAPONS DRIVEN BY AI

Technological developments have been used to wage war, as is far too frequently the case. Some people are eager to take action on AI before it's too late: Over 30,000 people, including robotics and AI experts, opposed the purchase of AI-powered autonomous weapons in an open letter published in 2016.

They added, "Whether to start a global AI arms race or to prevent it from starting is the key question for humanity today." "A global arms race is practically inevitable if any major military power pushes ahead with AI weapon development, and the endpoint of this technological trajectory is obvious: autonomous weapons will become the Kalashnikovs of tomorrow." Lethal Autonomous Weapon Systems, which find and eliminate targets independently while adhering to few rules, are the realization of this prophecy. Some of the most powerful countries in the world have succumbed to fear and aided in the emergence of a technological cold war as a result of the spread of powerful and sophisticated weapons.

Many of these new weapons are extremely dangerous for on-the-ground civilians, but the risk is increased when autonomous weapons end up in the wrong hands. Since hackers are skilled at launching a wide range of cyberattacks, it is not difficult to envision a hostile actor breaking into autonomous weaponry and causing a total apocalypse.

Artificial intelligence may wind up being used for malicious purposes if political rivalries and belligerent inclinations are not restrained. Some worry that if there's money to be earned, we'll keep pushing the boundaries of artificial intelligence

regardless of how many influential people warn about its risks.

AI'S WEAKENING OF ETHICS AND GOODWILL

Religious leaders are raising the alarm about the possible dangers of artificial intelligence, in addition to engineers, journalists, and politicians. During the Vatican summit in 2023 and his speech on the World Day of Peace in 2024, Pope Francis urged countries to draft and ratify a legally binding worldwide agreement that governs the advancement and application of artificial intelligence.

The misuse of AI, according to Pope Francis, could "create statements that at first glance appear plausible but are unfounded or betray biases," he said, stressing how this could bolster disinformation campaigns, mistrust of communications media, meddling in elections, and other activities, ultimately increasing the risk of "fueling conflicts and hindering peace."

These worries take on greater weight in light of the generative AI technologies' explosive growth. A lot of people have used technology to avoid writing projects, endangering both originality and academic integrity. Furthermore, as Pope Francis pointed out, biased AI might be used to decide if someone qualifies for a mortgage, employment, social aid, or political asylum, leading to potential injustices and discrimination.

THE IMPACT OF AI ON SOCIOECONOMIC INEQUALITY

Businesses may jeopardize their DEI ambitions through AI-powered hiring if they fail to recognize the innate biases ingrained in AI algorithms. AI's ability to quantify a candidate's qualities through speech and face analysis is still compromised by racial biases, perpetuating the very unfair hiring practices that companies claim to be doing away with.

Another reason to be concerned is the growing socioeconomic inequality brought about by AI-driven job losses, which exposes the class prejudices inherent in AI applications. Automation has resulted in salary losses of up to 70% for people who perform more manual, repetitive jobs; office and desk workers, on the other hand, have generally escaped the early effects of AI. Nonetheless, the growing usage of generative AI in offices is already having an impact on a variety of vocations, some of which may be more susceptible to pay or job loss than others.

Broad assertions that AI has somehow broken down social barriers or produced more jobs fall short of providing a full picture of its impacts. It is imperative to consider disparities based on racial, socioeconomic, and other characteristics. If not, it becomes more challenging to determine how automation and artificial intelligence assist some people and groups at the expense of others.

BIASES CAUSED BY AI

Different types of AI prejudice can also be harmful. Olga Russakovsky, a professor of computer science at Princeton University, told the New York Times that bias in AI extends far beyond issues of race and gender. Apart from data and algorithmic bias (which has the potential to "amplify" the former), artificial intelligence is created by humans, and humans are prejudiced by nature.

According to Russakovsky, "Most A.I. researchers are men, from specific racial demographics, who grew up in high socioeconomic areas, and who are primarily people without disabilities." "Because of our population's relative homogeneity, it can be difficult to think globally."

The narrow knowledge base of AI developers may help to explain why certain dialects and accents are difficult for voice recognition AI to understand, or why businesses overlook the potential repercussions of a chatbot posing as well-known historical individuals. More caution should be taken by corporations and developers to prevent the replication of strong biases and prejudices that endanger minority communities.

PRIVACY VIOLATIONS IN DATA USING AI TOOLS

Your data is being collected whether you've experimented with AI chatbots or AI face filters online, but where is it going and how is it being used? To personalize user experiences or to aid in training the AI models you're using; AI systems frequently gather personal data (especially if the AI tool is free). Given that one ChatGPT bug event in 2023 "allowed some users to see titles from another active user's chat history," data provided to an AI system may not even be deemed secure from other users. While several states in the US have laws protecting personal information, there isn't a specific federal legislation shielding citizens from the harm AI causes to their data privacy.

Artificial Intelligence for Social Surveillance
Apart from the existential risk it poses, Ford is particularly concerned about the negative impact AI will have on security and privacy. China's usage of facial recognition technology in workplaces, educational institutions, and other settings is a prime example. The Chinese government could be able to obtain enough information to keep tabs on someone's activities, relationships, and political

opinions in addition to tracking their whereabouts.

The use of predictive policing algorithms by US police agencies to identify crime hotspots is another example. The issue is that arrest rates, which disproportionately affect Black neighborhoods, have an impact on these algorithms. Following this, police forces intensify their efforts to target these communities, raising concerns about over-policing and the ability of self-declared democracies to prevent AI from becoming an instrument of authoritarianism.

According to Ford, "authoritarian regimes use it or will use it." "The question is, to what extent does it infiltrate democracies and Western nations, and what restrictions do we impose on it?"

AI-Powered Social Manipulation Techniques
Artificial intelligence also poses the risk of social manipulation. With politicians using platforms to advance their agendas, this worry has come to pass.

Ferdinand Marcos Jr., for instance, used a TikTok troll army to win over younger Filipino voters in the 2022 election.

One social networking site that uses AI algorithms is TikTok, which shows users content that is relevant to what they have already seen on the website. Critics point to this procedure and the algorithm's inability to weed out dangerous and false content, casting doubt on TikTok's capacity to shield its viewers from false information.

With AI-generated photos and videos, AI voice changers, and deep fakes penetrating the political and social domains, online media and news have become even more ambiguous. These technologies facilitate the creation of lifelike images, movies, and audio snippets, as well as the replacement of a figure's image in an already-existing image or video. This gives dishonest people a new channel to spread false information and propaganda for war, resulting in a situation where it can be extremely difficult to discern between reliable and inaccurate news.

Ford claimed that "nobody knows what's real and what's not." This ultimately results in a situation where you simply cannot trust what your own eyes and ears tell you, and you cannot rely on what we have traditionally thought to be the greatest available evidence. That will be a serious problem.

AI AUTOMATION-RELATED JOB LOSSES

Concerns about AI-powered job automation are growing as the technology is incorporated into sectors such as manufacturing, healthcare, and marketing. According to McKinsey, tasks that make up 30% of the hours worked in the U.S. industry by 2030 may be automated, leaving Black and Hispanic employees particularly vulnerable to the shift. According to Goldman Sachs, AI automation may result in the loss of 300 million full-time employees.

Future expert Martin Ford told Built-In, "The reason we have a low unemployment rate, which doesn't capture people that aren't looking for work, is largely because lower-wage service sector jobs have been pretty robustly created by this economy." However, "I don't think that's going to continue" given the growth of AI. Fewer people will be needed to perform the same work as AI robots grow in intelligence and dexterity. Even though it's predicted that artificial intelligence will generate 97 million new jobs by 2025, many workers won't be prepared for these technically demanding positions and risk falling behind if employers don't upskill their staff.

Absence of AI Explainability and Transparency
Even for individuals who deal closely with the technology, understanding AI and deep learning models can be challenging. Because of this, it becomes difficult to understand what data AI algorithms use or why they might make risky or biased decisions. As a result, there is a lack of openness regarding how and why AI draws its findings. Explainable AI has become popular as a result of these worries, but transparent AI systems are

still a way off from becoming standard.

Chapter 4

Techniques for Reducing Artificial Intelligence-Related Risks

In general, I believe that the best results will come from competition and crowdsourcing ideas. In reaction to such risks, there has been a lot of talk about regulating artificial intelligence. Even while I think most individuals have good intentions, I fail to see how this leads to a positive result. Similar to the drug war, excessive regulation often has the opposite effect of bringing undesirable conduct to a halt. However, I also think it's important to give voice to a wide range of viewpoints from those who hold different opinions than I do.

A few of these concepts may be debatable. I'm sure you'll find some excellent ideas and information to guide you on your journey towards discovering AI if you take a look.

Emphasis on Workforce Diversity and Ethics
I think ethical considerations should be taken into account when developing AI systems. Committees for ethical assessment should be established by organizations to examine AI projects, identify any prejudices, and guarantee equity. To lessen the risk of prejudice and discrimination in AI systems, efforts should also be made to diversify the workforce in this field.

Make AI Accountability and Transparency
Ensuring AI systems are transparent and accountable is one way to reduce possible risks related to artificial intelligence. This implies that the systems must be created in a way that makes it possible for users to comprehend how they operate and hold them responsible for their actions.

AI systems can be made transparent and accountable in several ways. Using explainable AI approaches is one approach. People can comprehend the decision-making process of AI systems thanks to explainable AI techniques. This can assist in locating and fixing any potential biases in the system.

Another technique to ensure that AI systems are transparent and accountable is to employ auditing and monitoring technologies. Tools for auditing and monitoring can be used to find possible issues with AI systems. They can also be used to monitor AI system performance and pinpoint areas in which they require improvement.

Put AI Governance and Regulation in Place

I think comprehensive frameworks for AI legislation and governance should be developed by governments and regulatory bodies. These frameworks ought to incorporate safety regulations, systems of accountability, data privacy laws, and ethical standards.

By establishing regulations that are explicit and enforceable, minimizing potential risks, and safeguarding the interests of both individuals and society at large, policymakers can guarantee that AI systems are developed and used responsibly.

Encourage Global Cooperation

International cooperation and standardization initiatives are essential for risk reduction given the global nature of artificial intelligence. To create worldwide norms, standards, and best practices for AI development and use, governments, organizations, and researchers should collaborate. This entails exchanging information, expertise, and data while promoting teamwork to tackle shared problems including prejudice, security, and privacy. International cooperation, in my opinion, may support the development of ethical AI practices, prevent the abuse of AI technology, and give a uniform, cross-national approach to AI.

Create and Implement AI Safety Guidelines

The creation and implementation of AI safety regulations is a practical means of reducing possible risks related to artificial intelligence (AI). These guidelines ought to be developed by a group of government, business, and academic experts on artificial intelligence.

The criteria would work to guarantee the safety, dependability, and transparency of AI system development. This will necessitate the creation of rules for the moral and responsible application of AI in a range of industries, including banking, healthcare, and transportation.

Furthermore, before being used, AI systems would need to go through extensive testing, including simulations and real-world scenarios, to guarantee conformity with these requirements. Sustaining adherence to these norms would also require a thorough system of impartial auditing and regulation.

Integrate Human Monitoring and Inspection

Combining human inspection and verification with artificial intelligence (AI) is one method for reducing possible dangers. This can entail using techniques for validation and verification, including post-deployment reviews or continuous testing, to have people examine the output of AI systems. For instance, a company might use non-experts to evaluate a sample of AI model outputs to determine whether or not the findings are reliable, ethical, and satisfactory. This would make it possible to swiftly identify and fix inaccurate outputs before they were shared more extensively.

Utilize AI as an Add-on

Instead of integrating AI into your operations entirely, use it as a supplement. Since artificial intelligence is still a young field, it's hard to say how the technology will eventually be integrated. For instance, even though AI can write blog posts fast, there's a good risk Google will someday penalize this kind of material. Your company will be in danger if you have become overly dependent on it. Use AI as a helper rather than a key component of your process to be safe.

Invest Resources in Human Monitoring

One recommended practice is to allot sufficient funds

for ongoing human monitoring and corrective action. There is a lot of risk associated with AI in terms of compliance and regulations. Furthermore, competitors in this industry can advance rapidly as well. To combat this, always keep choices actionable, but make sure monitoring is in place to adhere to regulatory requirements.

Stress Extensive Testing and Validation

Thorough testing and validation are a useful tactic for reducing possible dangers related to artificial intelligence. Establish thorough testing procedures to guarantee the correctness, dependability, and security of AI systems. Evaluate AI models, algorithms, and data sources in-depth to spot and address biases, weaknesses, and unforeseen outcomes. Continuous auditing and monitoring of AI systems can assist in locating problems and fixing them before they get worse.

Organizations may improve the reliability and quality of their AI systems, lower risks, and guarantee that AI technologies function as intended by prioritizing testing and validation.

Use AI Responsibly

The widespread use of AI and programs like ChatGPT calls for prudence. Among the causes are:

- ❖ **Lack of Sourcing:** AI systems frequently withhold information sources, which makes it challenging to track down and confirm the origins of data, impacting documentation and accountability.
- ❖ **Verification:** Users must independently verify any information that AI may present as it may be erroneous or out of current.
- ❖ **Data Security:** Because ChatGPT learns from user input, privacy problems are raised. Privacy might be jeopardized by entering proprietary, regulated, or personal data.

Although ChatGPT and other AI tools are beneficial, users should exercise caution. Carefully enter data into AI prompts, avoiding private or restricted information (such as PII or CUI). Adopt ethical procedures to maximize AI's potential while guaranteeing responsibility and safeguarding private data.

Create Regulatory Frameworks

Numerous nations have made artificial intelligence regulation a top priority, and the United States and the European Union are already developing more precise regulations to control the technology's increasing sophistication. To help responsibly govern AI use and development, the White House Office of Science and Technology Policy (OSTP) developed the AI Bill of Rights in 2022. Furthermore, in 2023, President Joe Biden signed an executive order mandating that federal agencies create new policies and procedures for AI security and safety.

Legal restrictions may potentially result in the prohibition of some AI technology, although this doesn't stop civilizations from researching the topic. "You control how AI is applied, but you don't stop advancements in fundamental technology. That would be foolish and possibly harmful, in my opinion. We determine when and where AI is acceptable— where we want it and where we don't. Additionally, many nations will choose differently.

SET AI STANDARDS AND HEARINGS IN ORGANIZATIONS

When incorporating AI into their operations, organizations can take a variety of actions at the corporate level. Companies can create procedures for keeping an eye on algorithms, gathering quality data, and interpreting AI algorithm results. Leaders may even include AI in regular business meetings and the company culture, setting guidelines for what constitutes appropriate AI technology.

Final Thought

But there ought to be more of an emphasis on the humanities' varied viewpoints in tech when it comes to society as a whole. "People from different backgrounds, genders, cultures, and socioeconomic groups, as well as those from other fields like economics, law, medicine, philosophy, history, sociology, communications, human-computer interaction, psychology, and Science and Technology Studies (STS)," the authors of AI must seek out their perspectives, experiences, and worries. The best way to develop responsible AI technology and make sure the field is still exciting for future generations of scientists is to strike a balance between human-centered thinking and high-tech innovation. It is important for leaders to constantly debate the risks associated with artificial intelligence so they can devise strategies for using the technology for good.

"I believe we can discuss all of these risks, as they are very real." However, AI will also be the most crucial instrument in our toolkit for resolving the most pressing issues at hand.

www.ingramcontent.com/pod-product-compliance
Lightning Source LLC
Chambersburg PA
CBHW070950220526
45471CB00007B/2972